DISCARD

The NEZ PERCES

People of the Far West

BY VICTORIA SHERROW

NATIVE AMERICANS
THE MILLBROOK PRESS
BROOKFIELD, CONNECTICUT

Cover photograph courtesy of Thomas J. Bacon

Photographs courtesy of the Thomas Gilcrease Institute of American History and Art: pp. 8, 49; Photo Researchers: p. 13 (© Boyd E. Norton); National Museum of the American Indian, Smithsonian Institution: p. 14; Oregon Historical Society: pp. 16 (neg. no. 4461), 41 (neg. no. 3219); The Capitol, Washington, D.C.: p. 18; Idaho State Historical Society: p. 20 (#63-221.25, photo by Jane Gay); American Museum of Natural History (neg. no. 317346, photo by Rodman Wanamaker): p. 22; National Museum of American Art, Washington, D.C., Art Resource/New York: p. 27; Bettmann Archive: pp. 32, 37, 45; Thomas Burke Memorial Washington State Museum: p. 33 (both); Washington State Historical Society: p. 42; © David R. Frazier: p. 54.

Map by Joe Le Monnier

Library of Congress Cataloging-in-Publication Data
Sherrow, Victoria.
The Nez Perces : people of the far west / by Victoria Sherrow.
p.   cm.—(Native Americans)
Includes bibliographical references (p. 61) and index.
Summary: Explores the early history and traditional life of the Nez Perce, their contacts with white explorers and settlers, the loss of their land, and their eventual surrender to reservation life.
ISBN 1-56294-315-4 (Lib. Bdg.)
1. Nez Perce Indians—Juvenile literature. [1. Nez Perce Indians. 2. Indians of North America.] I. Title. II. Series.
E99.N5S54   1994
978'.004974—dc20   93-15737   CIP   AC

Published by The Millbrook Press
2 Old New Milford Road
Brookfield, Connecticut 06804

Copyright © 1994 by Victoria Sherrow
Printed in the United States of America
All rights reserved
1 3 5 6 4 2

CONTENTS

Facts About the Traditional
Nez Perce Way of Life
7

Chapter One
Peaceful People of the Plateau
9

Chapter Two
Life in a Traditional Nez Perce Village
15

Chapter Three
Horses and Explorers
31

Chapter Four
Troubled Times
39

Chapter Five
The Nez Perces Today
51

A Nez Perce Creation Story:
The Heart of the Monster
56

Important Dates 58
Glossary 60
Bibliography 61
Index 63

The Nez Perces

FACTS ABOUT THE TRADITIONAL NEZ PERCE WAY OF LIFE

GROUP NAME:
Nimipu (or Chopunnish)

GEOGRAPHIC REGION:
Oregon, Idaho, and Washington

LANGUAGE:
Sahaptin (or Penutian)

HOUSE TYPE:
Lodges or bark-roofed longhouses;
later, buffalo hide Plains tipis

MAIN FOODS:
Salmon, large game, wild plants
(including camas bulbs, roots, and berries)

United States Army troops are shown surrounded by the Nez Perces in this painting by Olaf Seltzer titled "Battle of the Big Hole, 1877."

Chapter One

PEACEFUL PEOPLE OF THE PLATEAU

In August 1877, a band of weary Nez Perces made camp on the banks of Beaver Creek in Montana. For more than two months, these people had trudged over rough trails in bad weather trying to avoid United States Army troops. The soldiers had been ordered to take the Nez Perces to a reservation—land set aside for Indian settlement—far from their beloved homelands in Idaho and Oregon.

The Wallowa band of Nez Perces, led by its admired leader, Chief Joseph, did not want to go. Fighting broke out. The Wallowas set off on a harsh journey of some 1,700 miles (2,736 kilometers) to flee to Canada. Military troops chased them across valleys, canyons, and mountains.

That August day, the Indians thought they were several days ahead of the army, so they took time to hunt antelope and rest their horses. They went to sleep thinking they were safe. But soldiers from Helena, Montana, had spotted them. Colonel John Gibbon and his men attacked the camp at dawn. They shot and clubbed sleeping people and those who ran outside. Chief Joseph and Chief White Bird led the wounded and the women and children to safety. After a day-long battle, the Nez Perces drove the soldiers out of their camp.

The cost of this moment of victory was great. Eighty-nine people, including fifty women and children, lay dead. Colonel Gibbon later said, "Few of us will soon forget the wail of mingled grief, rage, and horror which came from the camp four or five hundred yards from us when the Indians returned to it and recognized their slaughtered warriors, women, and children."

The Nez Perces regrouped and headed for Yellowstone Park. From there, they crossed into Wyoming. Chased by twenty-one army units, they fled back to Montana. They were tired, and many were sick, so they rested at Snake Creek in the foothills of the Bear Paw Mountains. Canada lay only 40 miles (64 kilometers) away.

A second surprise attack, on September 30, destroyed their dream of freedom for good. Soldiers led by Colonel Nelson Miles attacked the camp. Chief Joseph rushed past armed men to join his family in his tent. "About seventy men, myself among them, were cut off," he said. "I thought of my wife and children, who were now surrounded by soldiers, and I resolved to go to them or die."

During a temporary lull in the fighting, the Nez Perces dug trenches in the frozen earth. They climbed inside them and waited, shivering, as the harsh winds of a blizzard raged around them. Once more, the bullets began to fly. Yellow Wolf, Chief

Joseph's nephew, described the mayhem: "Bullets from everywhere. A big gun throwing bursting shells. . . . Children were crying with cold. No fire. There could be no light. Everywhere the crying, the death wail. . . . All for which we had suffered lost!"

After five desperate days, the Nez Perces were finally defeated. During the Battle of Bear Paws, more than two hundred people had been killed in all, including Joseph's only brother, Ollokot. Chief Joseph surrendered rather than see more people die. He later mourned the loss of his "beautiful valley of winding waters," saying, "I love that land more than all the rest of the world."

The Nez Perces owned only a few horses when they were sent to a reservation in 1877. They had once been rich in land and livestock, and they had been free. The Nez Perces had a history of peace with whites. They had shown goodwill toward white explorers, traders, settlers, and missionaries. Until 1875, no Nez Perce had killed a white person. But growing numbers of settlers and gold seekers came to the Northwest. They wanted the land for their own. A series of broken promises by the U.S. government led the Nez Perces to fight for and lose their native lands.

ROOTS IN THE COLUMBIA PLATEAU ▪ For thousands of years, ancestors of the Nez Perces had lived on lands now part of Idaho, Oregon, and Washington. Small groups of people probably came from the Pacific Coast over a period of centuries. More powerful tribes may have pushed them east. They settled on the Columbia Plateau, which lies south of the Canadian border, east of the Cascade Mountains, and west of the Rocky Mountains. To the south is the Great Basin desert. The Plateau is a land of rivers, lush valleys, deep canyons, and snow-topped peaks.

The Nez Perces founded villages along the Snake, Clearwater, and Salmon rivers, which flow into the two main rivers in the area, the Columbia and the Fraser. Salmon and other fish in these streams were a major source of food for Plateau tribes. Archaeologists have made digs, or excavations, along the Columbia River. They have found fishnets, hooks, and fish bones that date back as far as 7500 B.C. Besides fishing, the Nez Perces hunted game and gathered edible plants that grew wild on their lands.

The language spoken by the Nez Perces came from a root called Sahaptin, or Shahaptin. Some of the nearby tribes—among them the Palouse, Cayuse, Walla Walla, Yakima, and Umatilla—used languages from this same root. The Flathead who lived to the northeast (in present-day Montana) and the Shoshoni to the south and southeast spoke different languages. Yet the tribes traded with each other, often through sign language. The Nez Perces also had contact with some of the Plains Indians who lived east of the Rockies.

As is true of most Native Americans, the name given to their tribe—Nez Perce—came from outsiders. They called themselves Chopunnish or Nimipu (nee-mee-poo), meaning "the people." French fur trappers who came to the area saw that some Nez Perces wore thin seashell ornaments in their noses. They had copied certain Columbia River Indians who pierced the wall between their nostrils. The trappers began calling them *Nez Percé* (nay-pearsay), which means "pierced nose" in French. Over the years, the name came to be pronounced "nezz purse." Actually, most Nez Perces did not pierce their noses.

The Snake River winds its way through Idaho before flowing into the Columbia Plateau in northern Oregon and Washington.

Nez Perce, meaning "pierced nose," was the name given to this group of Native Americans by French trappers. The nose ornament shown here is made of shell.

The Nez Perces were independent people who learned to meet their own needs. In the early 1700s they took advantage of the horses that wandered onto their lands and began to hunt buffalo on horseback. They bred fine horses and traded them for other goods. Besides being self-sufficient, the Nez Perces were known for their intelligence, their skills in public speaking, and their peaceful ways. They practiced a democratic style of government and honored the roles of men and women in community life.

Chapter Two

LIFE IN A TRADITIONAL NEZ PERCE VILLAGE

The Plateau was a region of great natural beauty during the changing seasons. But living there was hard. One problem facing the Nez Perces was finding enough food throughout the year. The day began when sunrise lit Montana's Bitterroot Mountains and glowed across the canyons of Idaho. As hawks and eagles circled above, a man with the job of town crier set off to awaken his fellow villagers. Women renewed the fires and cooked the morning meal—perhaps salmon or other fish, wild onions, and fried cakes made of huckleberries or camas bulb meal. Families drew near the fires to eat.

VILLAGES ▪ Nez Perce villages were nestled in canyons along rivers. Here, the people found good drinking water, fish and shellfish, and driftwood to use for fires and for building homes. It was easy to dig up the sandy soil with simple tools made from stone and bones.

This 1884 sketch shows a Nez Perce fishing camp along the shores of the Columbia River.

The deep canyons and creek bottoms gave some protection against the cold winters. But summer brought hot, dry weather to the riverbeds. Then the Nez Perces moved to camps high on plateaus 2,000 to 3,000 feet (608 to 912 meters) above the rivers. Edible plants grew on these plateaus, along with pines and fir trees.

There were between forty and sixty small Nez Perce villages located along the Snake, Lower Salmon, and Clearwater rivers.

The amount of food nearby determined how many people could live in one place. Among the villagers were husbands and wives, children, and a few older and widowed people. When a young woman married, she left her village to join her husband's.

Several Nez Perce villages made up a band. There were about seventy bands, with from twenty to three hundred people in each one. Bands belonged to either of two larger groups, depending on where they lived: the Upper Nez Perce and Lower Nez Perce. Each of these groups had its own leadership.

TRIBAL ORGANIZATION ▪ The Nez Perces were more tightly organized than their neighbors to the south. There was often a chief in charge of the entire tribe. However, he did not make decisions for all the others. An older man in the village, thought to be especially wise, served as an informal leader. These leaders could give advice or try to influence people. But they did not tell others what to do.

The Nez Perces believed that individuals had a right to make their own choices. At public council meetings, people discussed their concerns and tried to reach an agreement. People were allowed to move to a different village if they disagreed strongly with their group. A warrior could leave a battle if he chose not to fight any longer.

Although Nez Perce bands did not have a rigid government, they were bound together by a common language as well as beliefs and customs. Sometimes men and women from different bands married, which tied the various groups to one another. The bands also met every summer when they camped on the prairies to gather camas bulbs for food.

The Nez Perces held open council meetings where each member of the tribe was encouraged to speak.

HOMES AND PROPERTY ▪ The Nez Perces worked together to build communal homes, which were shared by a number of families. These lodges were about 15 feet (4.5 meters) wide and from 60 to 100 feet (18 to 30 meters) long. Up to thirty families might live in one longhouse.

The rectangular lodges were built around a central horizontal ridgepole. These longhouses had strong log frameworks, supported by short posts on each side and taller posts along the middle. Rafters stretched from the center to each side and were covered with layers of overlapping reed mats. Bulrushes and cattails were among the reeds and grasses used for the mats. Families had their own living areas and used mats for sleeping.

Winter nights were often icy cold. Warming fires were lit in the center of the lodges. Smoke holes were pierced in the center of each roof above the fire area. These holes let the smoke escape and let sunlight into the buildings during the day.

Some winter homes, called pithouses, were circular in shape. They were built over deep pits dug in the ground. People mounded dirt around the sides for added warmth. They made flat, domed roofs from wood rafters and poles. Holes in the roofs held ladders so that people could climb in and out.

▪ ▪ ▪

Besides their houses, villagers shared a sweathouse built near a stream. The Nez Perces liked to bathe daily and took steam baths for religious purposes. This small building was made of mud and grasses, then covered with mats. For a steam bath, rocks were first heated over a fire until they sizzled. Then they were put inside the sweathouse and water was poured on them to make steam. People often cooled off after a sweat bath by swimming in the nearby stream.

Sweathouse steam baths were part of the daily routine of the Nez Perces.

The Nez Perces believed that land was part of the Earth Mother, not personal property. Greed and selfishness were viewed as serious faults. Village land was shared by all. As a practical matter, families did use certain fishing areas on the river, passing this legacy from father to son.

FAMILY LIFE ■ Nez Perce women were treated with more respect than women of some other tribes. Their role as food providers gave them added importance. Women expressed their opinions and could disagree with their fathers or husbands. They chose the men they wished to marry.

There were more women than men, so men might have more than one wife at a time. This let the tribe produce more children. More people could share the work that must be done, including protecting themselves from enemies. Women shared the jobs of food gathering and child rearing with other wives. It was a tribal rule that wives must get along and treat each other well.

The Nez Perces valued a happy family life. Many of the villagers were related to each other, so extended families were common. Inside the longhouses, people cooperated so that all could prosper. They tried to live together in harmony.

RAISING CHILDREN ▪ The birth of a baby was a joyful event. Nez Perce infants spent their first months strapped onto cradleboards. These wooden boards were often padded with animal skins or fluffy plant materials. Some had fancy painted designs and footrests and hoops to protect the infant's head. As mothers did their daily chores, they carried their babies along. The sturdy cradleboard could be set against a tree trunk, wall, or rock as the mother cooked, wove baskets, or gathered plants. When babies were ready to crawl and walk, they were freed from their cradleboards and allowed to play on the ground.

Children were not strictly disciplined by adults. Grandparents played a large part in teaching the young what was expected of them. The children learned the customs and values of their group and were expected to behave properly. A child who misbehaved faced the scorn of fellow villagers. It was more comfortable to obey the rules than to be rejected or criticized by

A Nez Perce mother holds her baby in a cradleboard.

others. Village elders taught them Nez Perce history and legends. Some stories were funny or entertaining, while others held lessons about the evil of greed and the virtues of courage and honor. In everyday life the need to respect nature was stressed. Children learned that human beings, plants, animals, water, and earth were all part of one inseparable whole, meant to live in harmony.

Mothers taught their daughters the special duties and skills of Nez Perce women. Young men learned from their fathers how to hunt, fish, and make tools—the spears, bows, arrows, fishing nets, and knives they needed for hunting and protection. They learned how to stalk animals in the forest by following a trail and imitating the sounds of the animals. By their late teens, boys were permitted to fight as warriors. Still, the main job of both men and women was the continual search for enough food throughout the year.

PLATEAU FISHING ▪ Nez Perce fishermen kept busy from May through November when millions of salmon from the Pacific Ocean darted through the Plateau rivers. There were also trout, sturgeon, and other fish. Fish was eaten fresh when in season and was also stored for winter use.

Eagerly, the fishermen waited each spring for the different kinds and sizes of salmon—chinook, sockeye, humpback, and silver coho. These fish moved from the ocean into smaller streams every year in order to spawn, or mate, in the same gravel beds. Their offspring swam back to the ocean and, once grown, they returned to spawn as their parents had before them.

The Nez Perces invented several clever ways to snare their slippery catch. Sometimes they waded into the water and used lines and hooks, spears, or even bows and arrows, to kill them. Other times, they laid traps of willow brush and poles across a stream when the salmon were expected. Some bold fishermen waited on ledges over swift-moving streams. They leaned over to catch the passing fish with nets made of plant fibers.

After being caught, the fish were cut open and cleaned. Some were eaten, while a good many were sun-dried on large wooden racks set up beside the rivers. Others were preserved by smoking them over the fire. During the winter, the dried and smoked fish were eaten or traded for other foods or goods.

During a good year, nearly 80 percent of the food supply might be fish. The Nez Perces did not raise crops through farming. A poor fishing season meant they would have to work extra hard to find enough game and wild plants to survive.

GATHERING PLANTS ■ Through the centuries, the Nez Perces learned to eat many plants that grew wild on the Plateau. These included berries, carrots and other roots, onions and other bulbs, nuts, grasses, herbs, and fruits. Many could also be dried and stored for winter meals. Among the seasonal harvest were pink-flowered bitterroots and starchy camas lily bulbs. Huckleberries, serviceberries, currants, rose hips, and mountain sunflower stems added welcome color and flavor to their diet.

Of all the plant foods, the camas bulb was especially important. Camas belongs to the lily family and shows its blue flowers in early summer. The Idaho Nez Perces camped every summer at Camas Prairie and Weippe, where these lilies carpeted the ground by June or July.

About three hundred to four hundred people gathered in each camp for six weeks. Women used curved digging sticks made from willow branches to gather the bulbs. As the women dug, the men hunted, gathered firewood, guarded the campsite, and made new tools.

Summer was also a happy social time. People got to see friends and family members from other villages. They shared news of the past year and chatted as they worked. Young people met others whom they might want to marry. Dancing, races, and games gave people of all ages time to have fun and get to know each other.

Pinecone Games

Nez Perce children spent much of their time doing chores. But like children everywhere, they found time to play. With no toy stores of ready-made playthings, they invented many games using things from nature. One item they could get easily on parts of the Plateau was pinecones. Children used the cones to play catch or in contests to see who could throw the farthest or the highest. Sometimes, they found a tree with a hole in the side and tried to toss cones into the hole from different distances.

One pinecone tossing game involved a hoop. Hoops were made from long grasses, reeds, or branches from willows or other trees that could be bent into a circle. These hoops ranged in size from 12 to 24 inches (30 to 61 centimeters) across.

To play, the children placed the hoop a certain number of feet away from the throwing line. They stood behind the line and tried to toss cones into the hoop. As the hoop was moved farther and farther away, it took more skill to get the cones inside. Children changed the rules of these games to keep them interesting. They might play in teams. Sometimes all the players had to throw underhand. Or they might get different numbers of points, depending on where their cones landed inside the hoop.

You can play your own pinecone tossing game with a plastic hoop or even a box. Place the box on the ground or hang it from a tree with a rope. Players score by getting their cones inside the box.

Late summer also brought berries. Some were dried and mixed with dough to make cakes for winter. By August, it was time to carry the harvest to the village. A large crop might require villagers to travel back and forth two or three times loaded with bundles of bulbs and cakes.

HUNTING FOR MEAT AND FOWL ▪ Fish and plants could not feed the Nez Perces all year long. They hunted game and fowl, including ducks and geese that lived along the rivers and lakes. Antelope roamed the mountainsides, while deer, elk, and moose were found in the woods and meadows. Mountain sheep and goats grazed on higher ground. Even black bears were killed and eaten.

The men found creative ways to trap and catch game. Before the Nez Perces began to use horses, they tracked animals on foot. They used nets to trap small game like rabbits. Hunters dressed in deerskins and antlers so as not to scare their prey. To catch ducks and geese, they waded slowly along in the water with gourds covering their heads so they would not look like men.

In the winter, hunters put on snowshoes made from plant fibers and braved icy winds to kill a deer or elk. But they relied mainly on the food they got during the warmer seasons to survive through the cold months when game was scarce.

HOUSEHOLD GOODS AND TOOLS ▪ The Nez Perces made skillful use of the raw materials in their world. They wove the stems of cattails and tule plants into mats. Women twisted and wound fibers into strong carrying bags, and men made plant-fiber nets for hunting and fishing.

This 1832 painting by George Catlin depicts a Nez Perce wearing ceremonial clothing. Everyday dress was likely to be simple buckskin cloths and beaded moccasins.

Unlike many other Native Americans, the Nez Perces did not have clay, so they wove cedar roots into watertight baskets to use as cookware and containers. Women cooked by tossing red-hot stones inside a basket filled with food and covering the top. Large baskets were used to gather roots and plants. Others stored water.

Men used stones and minerals to make arrowheads, spearpoints, knives, and tools to scrape animal hides. From mountain sheep horn they created dippers, bowls, drinking horns, and spoons. Fine hunting bows were carved from this horn, too. Deer sinew—strong bands of tissue that connect bone to muscle—made the string. A finished bow was sturdy enough to shoot a 3-foot-long (1-meter) arrow.

The centers of cedar and pine logs were burned out to make dugout canoes. Paddles or poles moved the canoe along. The Nez Perces fished from canoes and used them to travel to nearby villages.

SPIRITUAL BELIEFS ▪ The Nez Perces believed in a great spirit called *Hanyawat*, or Old One, who created all things. Old One had a helper, Coyote, who was supposed to keep evil spirits from causing too much trouble in the world. From an early age, children heard many Coyote stories. Sometimes Coyote was a fine, helpful spirit; other times he was quite mischievous. Besides Coyote, there were different spiritual helpers with special jobs. Helper Grizzly Bear is said to have brought huckleberries to the Nez Perces.

The Nez Perces had fairly simple customs and beliefs. To show thankfulness, they held ceremonies for the first run of salmon each spring and the first wild fruits and meats. They believed in killing animals or plants only if they were needed. People were supposed to treat others as they themselves wished to be treated. Elders were respected, and ancestral graves were sacred. The dead were said to watch over the living to be sure they behaved with honor and were honest in words and deeds.

Spiritual leaders and healers—shamans—got their power from supernatural beings. Both men and women could be shamans. They tried to cure illness with special dancing, chanting, and smoking rituals.

Young Nez Perces sought their own spirit guardian in order to gain spirit power, called *tiwatitmas*. Spirit helpers were thought to help people throughout life and to aid men in hunting and war.

Many ten-year-old children set off on a spirit, or vision, quest. An adult tied a sacred object, such as a feather, to the children's clothing. They walked alone to the mountains, where they built a fire that was to burn at all times. They prayed and fasted as they watched the sinking sun. The children continued to face that same direction until dawn, when they turned around to see the sun rise. They repeated this pattern the next night and day, taking no food or water. The vision was supposed to come in animal form.

In the meantime, the child's family was preparing a feast back home. Family and friends ate with the returning child, but no one spoke about the fast in the mountains. Young Nez Perces might embark on spirit quests several times more by age fifteen. Throughout life, spirits might also "speak" to people in their dreams.

When someone died, the Nez Perces held mourning and burial ceremonies. They washed the corpse and dressed it in new clothing. The dead were buried outside the village with their heads pointing downstream. Death was seen as the natural end of life, after which people joined the spirit world and watched over the living.

■ ■ ■

For thousands of years, the Nez Perces followed their orderly way of life. They moved with the seasons and lived in harmony with nature. In the 1700s, strangers who followed very different customs began to come to the Plateau. By the 1800s thousands of settlers had moved to the area and claimed Nez Perce land. These white people thought they had a right to take the land and to impose their own beliefs on its native inhabitants. The lifestyle of the Nez Perces was to change greatly and against their will.

Chapter Three

HORSES AND EXPLORERS

Horses were introduced to America by the Spaniards, who rode on horseback into the Southwest in 1540. Indians there became familiar with horses and eventually raised their own. Some horses ran off into the wild. Perhaps the Nez Perces tamed the stray horses that wandered north. Or they may have gotten horses from their southern neighbors, the Shoshonis, who raised herds of them on grazing areas in what is now Montana. In any case, the Nez Perces had their own horses by about 1720.

Horses must have delighted people who had never seen them before. The Nez Perces learned to raise, train, and ride them well. Better transportation meant more contact with other tribes, such as the Cayuse, Walla Walla, Yakima, Palouse, Flathead, and coastal Indians. Nez Perces could now travel more easily to the large fairs held at Celilo Falls and The Dalles, both on the Columbia River.

In 1910 the American Tobacco Company capitalized on Americans' interest in the West and in Native Americans by issuing this trade card titled "Capturing a Wild Horse."

The Nez Perces traded a number of their goods, including tanned sheepskins and deerskins, baskets and carrying bags woven of reeds and grasses, and Plateau foods—dried berries, kouse roots, and camas. They traded the strong bows, eating utensils, and containers they crafted so painstakingly from sheep horn.

If they did not catch enough fish in the summer, the Nez Perces might exchange their goods for dried salmon. They also prized the seashells from the Pacific coast that they used as ornaments and decorations. As coastal goods moved east to Plateau Indians, they could trade those things, in turn, to Plains Indians. From the Sioux and other Plains tribes that lived east of them, the Nez Perces acquired fine feathers, animal skins, and warm buffalo robes.

With horses, the Nez Perce could hunt buffalo themselves. This gave them another source of meat to add to their diet. Horses also made it easier to carry loads of meats and plants home after hunting and gathering trips.

Nez Perce women used beads to decorate clothing, such as these moccasins and this cone-shaped hat. Many colorful beads were obtained through trade with coastal or Plains Indians.

Along with meat, buffaloes provided hides for clothing and shelter. The Nez Perces began making buffalo tipis similar to those of the Plains Indians. The hides were sewn into a semicircle, then hung around a frame made of wood poles. These strong tents could be carried from place to place.

Horses brought more contact within the tribe itself. Nez Perces could visit each others' villages faster and more easily. On horseback, people rode from more distant places than ever before to attend the annual camas gathering at Weippe Meadow and Camas Prairie. Young people married others living farther away. Marriage to non–Nez Perces increased, too, as they met more people from other tribes.

With this new mobility, conflicts increased, too. Fights broke out between tribes who were now in greater contact. Sometimes, people fought over the rights to hunt and fish on certain lands. Nez Perce men spent more time preparing for war and learning how to defend their people. The tribe began to stress bravery in battle, and warriors had more prestige than in past years.

EXPERT HORSE BREEDERS ▪ The Nez Perces developed their own methods of selective breeding. That is, they chose which horses should have offspring, and prevented sick or weak horses from reproducing. This enabled them to raise better horses than many other tribes. Among the breeds they raised was the handsome spotted Appaloosa. The Nez Perces are often pictured riding Appaloosas. But there is no proof that they preferred them to other breeds.

With rich grazing lands, the tribe could raise more horses than it needed. They sold about six hundred horses each year, keeping those they liked best for breeding. People prized Nez Perce horses, known for their superior size and strength. Trading horses gave the Nez Perces a steady source of wealth.

EARLY CONTACTS WITH WHITES ▪ White fur trappers from Canada and Europe began coming to Nez Perce country in the mid-1700s. Lustrous beaver pelts were in demand in both Europe and the American colonies. They were made into such things as tall hats for men, coat collars and trims, and handheld muffs. Indians living in the Northeast had been trapping beavers to trade with whites for more than two hundred years. Now people flocked to the Northwest, eager to get the large numbers of beaver that lived in the region's streams.

The Nez Perces did not trade many furs with the white men who came to their land. They preferred to trade their horses for knives, blankets, and other goods. Their early meetings were peaceful. The white men were not taking things the Nez Perces needed. They did not think that these few white men would pose a problem. After all, there was plenty of unsettled land.

FIRST EXPLORERS ▪ In the late 1700s, dramatic changes took place in North America. The American colonies defeated Great Britain to gain their independence. The new United States founded a government, and more Europeans came to live in America. Many chose to go west rather than settle near the Atlantic coast.

In 1803 the United States government arranged a massive land deal called the Louisiana Purchase. It paid France three cents an acre for the lands that lay between the Mississippi River and the Rocky Mountains, called the Louisiana Territory. The

French had claimed ownership of this area—which covered almost half of the entire United States—after defeating Spain, the European country that had controlled it before them. Native Americans had lived on these lands for thousands of years, but they did not have a voice in the decisions that would change their lives forever.

In September 1805, some explorers arrived at an Indian village of mat-covered lodges on the Clearwater River in Idaho. These white men had traveled hundreds of miles, crossing the snowy Bitterroot Mountains. They were sick and hungry. Their horses were worn out.

The explorers were members of the famous Lewis and Clark expedition. President Thomas Jefferson had organized the group to explore the Louisiana Territory and keep detailed records of what they saw there. Good luck had brought them to Nez Perce land, which William Clark described in his diary as "beautiful country."

Clark and his men had been eating bear grease, candle wax, and horsemeat to stay alive. The friendly Nez Perces fed the strangers and cared for their horses. In his diary, William Clark wrote that the Nez Perces "gave us a small piece of buffalow meat, some dried salmon beries and roots in different states. . . . I found myself verry unwell . . . from eateing the fish and roots too freely."

The explorers spent six weeks in the village. The Indians made five dugout canoes and helped them plan a route to their destination, the Pacific Ocean. They drew maps of the area's waterways and canyons with charcoal on a piece of whitened elkskin. The grateful explorers left their horses and some goods

Relations between the Nez Perces and the exploring party led by Lewis and Clark were friendly.

with the villagers. They took Nez Perce food and other supplies as they set off down the Clearwater River.

The Nez Perces welcomed the explorers again when they returned from the Pacific Coast to get their horses in April 1806. Both groups expressed their hope for peaceful relations in the future. Clark gave the Nez Perce leaders bronze medals and U.S. flags as signs of friendship before the whites left for St. Louis.

NEW TRADE GOODS ▪ Despite these peaceful visits, whites had introduced western Indians to a new kind of deadly weapon: guns. By 1800, the Blackfeet tribe of Montana had guns. They were a large, aggressive tribe and enemies of the Nez Perces.

Hunting in Montana was even more dangerous after the Blackfeet had muskets.

Nez Perce leaders realized their usual weapons were not enough protection against these quick and deadly arms. They sent a group of men to some Mandan villages in 1805 to trade for guns. The Mandans had traded with whites for some guns, and they gave the Nez Perce six of them.

A new trading post opened near the mouth of the Little Spokane River in 1809. The Nez Perces traded horses for guns, metal items, and cloth. Steel blades were sharper and lasted longer than stone ones. Metal cooking pots and steel sewing needles were also valued. Wool blankets made warm robes and bedding. In wet or hot weather, wool and cotton clothing felt more comfortable than leather. Some items were acquired for sheer pleasure—mirrors, beads, brass bells, ribbons, and pipe tobacco that had been grown in the East.

Whites brought other things even more harmful than guns. They carried unfamiliar diseases to which Indians had no natural resistance. Many Native Americans died from such illnesses as measles, smallpox, typhoid fever, and tuberculosis.

Besides diseases, there were social problems. Fighting among tribes increased as they competed with each other for the rich fur trade. From time to time, whites and Indians married. Their children suffered when neither group would accept them.

Problems arose among Indians and American traders. They did not understand each other's cultures or languages well. As the 1800s wore on, conflicts grew as more whites came to Nez Perce country, with tragic results for the tribe.

Chapter Four

TROUBLED TIMES

During the 1800s, the Nez Perces struggled to get along with the increasing numbers of whites who came to the Plateau. They were courteous to Christian missionaries and worked hard to come to terms with government officials who claimed their lands. Over and over, their trust was betrayed as treaties and promises were broken.

CHRISTIAN MISSIONS ▪ By the 1830s, missionaries began coming to the Northwest to convert Native Americans to Christianity. The Nez Perces had heard about the white man's religion and were curious to learn more. They had seen white medicines that seemed to work like magic. They liked the whites' "talking papers" (letters). By marking the paper a certain way, whites could send messages that others could understand.

Some Nez Perce leaders thought that learning the white man's magic would make them more powerful. Perhaps white religion held ideas they might add to theirs.

Missionaries Henry and Eliza Spalding arrived in 1836 to set up a Christian mission at Lapwai Creek, the first on Nez Perce land. The Spaldings organized the Indians to build a log cabin and schoolhouse. Eliza Spalding learned the Nez Perce language in order to translate the Bible and teach reading and writing.

Tu-eka-kas, the respected leader of the Wallowa Nez Perces, moved to the Spalding mission in 1838. He studied the white man's "spirit law" and invited Spalding to visit the Wallowa Valley in 1839. Tu-eka-kas and his wife were baptized, and, later, so were their two sons. Tu-eka-kas took the Christian name Joseph. His son, born in 1840 in Oregon, also took this name. He would later become Chief Joseph.

The Indians disliked Henry Spalding's strict rules. Spalding forbade them to wear clothing that left their legs or arms bare or to dance, hold traditional feasts, race horses, or hunt buffalo. The Nez Perces were furious when Spalding whipped Indians who disobeyed him. They were used to thinking for themselves and making decisions after discussing matters together. Although they welcomed the chance to hear the whites' ideas, the Nez Perces had not intended to put the whites in charge of their lives.

YEARS OF CHANGE AND BROKEN PROMISES ■ More missionaries, Catholic and Protestant, followed the Spaldings to the Northwest. Sometimes different religions set up missions near each other and competed for followers. White settlers were en-

Christian missionary Henry Spalding. Disagreements with Spalding eventually led many Nez Perces to leave his mission.

couraged to move west, too. The Nez Perces did not then know about Manifest Destiny—a widely accepted idea that the United States should expand its borders until it included all land between the Atlantic and Pacific oceans.

By 1842, thousands of settlers were living in the Northwest. They were not as afraid of hostile attacks as settlers were in other regions of the frontier because missionaries had always been safe on Nez Perce lands. In 1843 wagon trains of settlers moved into Oregon Territory to farm the rich soil.

At the 1855 Walla Walla Council, the Nez Perces were pressured by the governor of the Northwest Territory, Isaac Stevens, to give up their land and move to reservations.

In 1855 Isaac Stevens, the new governor of the Northwest Territory, asked the Indians in that region to meet with him. He said they must leave their lands and move to small reservations. In return, Stevens offered them homes, livestock, schools, and goods from the "Great Father" in Washington, D.C.

The Nez Perces were skeptical. But how could they resist when there were so many more whites than Indians? They finally signed the Walla Walla Treaty. Tu-eka-kas was told that his band would have a reservation that included the Wallowa Valley and their other major campsites. Stevens promised, "So long as the sun travels across the sky shall this reservation belong to the Indians and no white man shall be allowed on it." The Nez Perces hoped that giving up some of their land would satisfy the whites.

Their hopes were soon shattered. Stevens had said the Nez Perces could stay where they were for a few years, but white settlers began arriving on their land only a few days after the treaty was signed. Then, in 1860, gold was found on their reservation. At first, a few gold prospectors came and did not bother the Nez Perces much. Then miners, merchants, and settlers streamed in. Whites took their horses and livestock. The Nez Perces tried to guard their land and keep people from building homes on it. When they asked government officials for help, they got none.

Instead, the officials asked the Nez Perces to give up more of their land. In 1863, several chiefs who led bands of Upper Nez Perces signed away larger areas of land. They moved to the Lapwai Reservation in Idaho. More than half of the Nez Perce chiefs refused to move. They called the treaty a "Thief Treaty."

Tu-eka-kas was among those who did not sign the 1863 treaty. He warned his sons, Joseph and Ollokot, not to take any gifts because it might look as if they had sold their land. Young Joseph (Hin-mah-too-yah-lat-kekt) was then a tall, dignified man of twenty-three. When Tu-eka-kas lay dying in 1871, he told him, "Never forget my dying words. This country holds your father's body. Never sell the bones of your father and mother." Joseph later said, "I pressed my father's hand and told him that I would protect his grave with my life. My father smiled and passed away to the spiritland."

CHIEF JOSEPH ▪ When Joseph became chief of the Wallowa Nez Perces in 1871, relations with whites had worsened. Years later, Joseph recalled, "They stole a great many horses from us and we could not get them back because we were Indians. . . . They drove off a great many of our cattle. Some white men branded our young cattle so that they could claim them. We had no friends who would plead our cause before the [white] law councils."

The Nez Perces angrily ordered the settlers to leave. By now, they had rejected white ways and religion. A new Indian religion called the Dreamer faith spread from the Columbia River tribes to the Nez Perces. Dreamers believed that one day Indians would again live free as their ancestors had.

A new 1873 agreement with the U.S. government let the Wallowa band keep most of their land and said white settlers must leave. Just one year later, this agreement was voided; whites were told that the Wallowa Valley was again open for settlement.

White officials then told Joseph his band must go to Lapwai. Joseph protested that the reservation was too small for the people and their animals. At a meeting in Oregon, he said, "The white man has no right to come here and take our country. This land has always belonged to my people."

Joseph reminded government agents that his band had never sold its land or agreed to give it up. For a while, some officials agreed. The Bureau of Indian Affairs said that because Joseph's people had not signed the 1863 treaty, the land was still theirs.

But white settlers stayed in Wallowa. More came, building farms, ranches, roads, and bridges. In 1875, President Ulysses S. Grant decided to disregard all claims by the Wallowa Nez

Chief Joseph of the Nez Perces.

Perces. He signed a statement that gave the valley to white homesteaders.

To avoid problems, Joseph moved his band to a smaller section of the valley. But the two groups clashed. White ranchers killed a young Nez Perce who they said had stolen their horses. Joseph tried to calm his people to prevent more violence. Nervous settlers asked the U.S. Army for troops to protect them if fighting broke out.

In May 1877, General Oliver Howard was told to take the Nez Perces to the reservation. A Civil War hero, Howard was regarded as fair and sympathetic. In a letter to Washington, he had written, "I think it is a great mistake to take from Joseph and his band of Nez Perce Indians that valley." But when his commanders said the band must be at Lapwai within thirty days, Howard told Joseph, "the Indians must go . . . my orders are plain."

The Nez Perces were stunned. A month was not nearly enough time to gather thousands of horses and cattle and other goods. They would have to cross the Snake River in late spring when it was flooded with melting snow from the mountains. Still, the chiefs did not want war. The whites had far more soldiers and better weapons. Joseph calmed the young warriors who told him they would rather "fight than be driven like dogs from the land where they were born."

After packing what they could, the Wallowas set out across the muddy land. The Snake River was treacherous. The people built rafts for infants, the elderly, and household goods. Young men swam beside the rafts to push them across the swollen river. Some horses and cattle drowned, but all the people reached the shore.

They climbed a steep hill before crossing the Salmon River, which was also flooded. After scaling a rocky canyon, they came to an ancient Nez Perce meeting place near Tolo Lake. They would camp there before the long ride to the Lapwai Reservation.

THE NEZ PERCE WAR ▪ All their plans changed on the morning of June 13. Nez Perce warriors knew of a rancher who had killed one of their fathers, and other whites had beaten one of their friends. They decided to seek revenge. During two days of raids, they killed eighteen or nineteen settlers.

Joseph had crossed the river to butcher beef. When he got back, the camp was in an uproar. The Nez Perce chiefs knew white soldiers would come after the warriors. The group moved to White Bird Canyon where they could protect themselves. Later, Joseph recalled, "I was deeply grieved. I would have given my own life if I could have undone the killing of white men by my people. I know that our young men did a great wrong, but I ask, 'Who was to blame?'"

Chief Joseph wanted to avoid war. Early on June 17, Nez Perce scouts signaled that white soldiers were coming. When the soldiers rode into the canyon, six Indians rode to meet them carrying a white flag of truce. Despite the flag, a soldier fired two shots at the riders. Indians hiding in the rocks returned fire. Twelve soldiers were shot from their horses; the others fled. More shooting left thirty-four soldiers dead and two Indians wounded.

After that, the Wallowas decided to flee to Canada. Most of them were women, children, and old men. They crossed rough mountains and canyons in Idaho, Wyoming, and Montana as they stayed two days ahead of General Howard.

Rains and mud slowed their trip up the steep Lolo Trail and over the Bitterroot Mountains. An army fort blocked the trail through the Bitterroot Valley. On July 27, the captain of the fort refused to let them pass into the valley. The Nez Perces had to make their way along a dangerous ledge. Bypassing the fort, they crossed the valley where local shopkeepers sold them supplies.

For about 1,700 miles (2,720 kilometers), two army units chased the Nez Perces. About 250 Nez Perces faced 2,000 soldiers and volunteers in thirteen battles. Yet the outnumbered Indians won or held their own each time. Americans read about the Nez Perces and expressed sympathy for them. Newspaper articles called Joseph the "Indian Napoleon." He later said, "The Great Spirit puts into the heart and head of man how to defend himself."

On October 5, after the Nez Perces were overtaken at the Bear Paw Mountains of Montana, Joseph surrendered to Colonel Nelson Miles. Only 87 men were still alive. Joseph knew that the 184 women and 147 children might soon die in the cold dugouts. That morning, Joseph came out of the camp and rode toward the soldiers. He handed Miles his rifle and delivered this eloquent speech of surrender:

> *I am tired of fighting. Our chiefs are killed. . . . It is cold and we have no blankets. The little children are freezing to death. My people, some of them, have run away to the hills and have no blankets, no food. . . . Hear me, my chiefs. I am tired. My heart is sick and sad. From where the sun now stands, I will fight no more forever.*

Miles told Joseph the Nez Perces would be able to keep their remaining livestock and go to Lapwai. But he could not keep his

This painting by Olaf Seltzer titled "Chief Joseph's Surrender to Colonel Nelson A. Miles" shows the great chief delivering his surrender speech to his Nez Perce followers.

promise. Officials ordered Miles to take the Nez Perces to North Dakota. They were then moved to Kansas, where the polluted drinking water and unhealthy conditions caused people to die of diseases. By 1878, seventy more people had died from illness. In 1880, they were moved again, this time to Indian territory in Oklahoma.

Joseph went to Washington, D.C., to ask the president to help his people. Still, the Nez Perces were not allowed to return to the Northwest until 1885. Instead of Lapwai, Joseph's Wallowa group was taken to the Colville Reservation in Washington. "When will the white man learn to tell the truth?" Joseph often asked.

Chief Joseph never gave up his hope of returning to the Wallowa Valley. In 1900 he asked to buy a small piece of land there, but the whites in the area refused. After visiting his father's grave, Joseph returned sadly to his tipi at Colville. He died at age sixty-four on September 21, 1904. At his funeral, his nephew, Yellow Wolf, said, "Joseph is dead but his words are not dead. His words will live forever." Lieutenant Wood, who had seen Joseph surrender at the Bear Paws, wrote, "I think that, in his long career, Joseph cannot accuse the Government of one single act of justice."

The injustices suffered by the Nez Perces were typical of those suffered by other tribes. During the 1850s, the U.S. government gained 157 million acres (64 million hectares) of Indian lands. Many treaties were signed, but few were honored. Chief Joseph was a powerful spokesperson for all Native Americans. His efforts sparked some whites to ask for fairer government policies during the 1900s.

Chapter Five

NEZ PERCES TODAY

As the 1900s began, the loss of their lands and old ways of life brought economic hardships to the Nez Perces. They lacked housing, quality food, and health care. Isolation and discrimination against Native Americans added more obstacles. But the Nez Perces had long been known for their resourcefulness. They organized their tribal government and developed new sources of income as they faced the challenges of the twentieth century.

AN EVEN CHANCE ▪ Chief Joseph had spoken about the need to give his people "an even chance to live and grow" as Indians, not whites. He said, "Let me be a free man—free to travel, free to stop, free to work, free to trade where I choose, free to choose my own teachers, free to follow the religion of my fathers, free to think and talk and act for myself—and I will obey every law or submit to the penalty."

More than twenty years passed before this idea began to take hold. The Snyder Act of 1924 gave Native Americans full U.S. citizenship. In 1934 the Indian Reorganization Act recognized their right to form their own tribal governments and to follow the religions they chose. The Nez Perce Tribe of Idaho became a self-governing body in 1948 with its own constitution and bylaws.

RIGHTING OLD WRONGS ▪ By 1946, the U.S. government had set up the Indian Claims Commission to hear complaints by Native Americans. Tribes could file claims if they could prove their land had been taken illegally or that the government had paid them less than the fair market value. Tribes could also ask the government to pay them for property that had been taken from them without permission.

The Nez Perces filed a legal claim to recover money for lands taken in violation of treaties and for the gold that was removed from their land. They spent months studying old maps and historical documents to find the exact boundaries of their ancient lands. They worked hard to figure out how much gold the many prospectors might have removed during the mining years. In 1959 the Claims Commission said that the government owed the Nez Perces close to $20 million.

The Nez Perces at Kamiah reservation in Idaho used some of this money to build tribal-run businesses and a large youth center. The center included offices and rooms and equipment for group meetings, clubs, social events, dances, and sports events.

The Nez Perces have joined with other Native Americans in the Northwest to protect their treaty fishing rights. Together with Umatilla, Yakima, and Warm Springs reservation members, they formed the Columbia River Inter-Tribal Fish Commission. Fishing has continued to be an important source of food and income for the Nez Perces.

CHANGING WAYS OF LIFE ■ On the three reservations—Kamiah and Lapwai in Idaho and Colville in Washington—the Nez Perces have developed other businesses. Besides restaurants, hotels, and retail stores, they run breeding ranches for Appaloosas and other horses.

At Lapwai, the tribe owns 86,500 acres (35,000 hectares), just 13 percent of what they were promised in 1863. They run retail stores, a timber business, and a limestone quarry. Some of them work at nearby Nez Perce National Historical Park, which was founded in 1965.

With 1 million acres (approximately a half-million hectares), Colville is the largest of the reservations. The Nez Perces live here with about ten other tribes. There are feasts and ceremonies, traditional dances, craft fairs, and much visiting among relatives. Colville has a timber industry with planned cutting of various types and ages of trees.

At times, unemployment has been a problem. During the Great Depression of the 1930s, people could not get jobs helping at local farms and orchards. Many Indians sold their cherished family possessions, such as feathered headdresses, baskets, beaded bags, and shell ornaments so they could buy food.

Since the mid-1950s, unemployment has been less of a problem. One reason is that the Nez Perces have shown a strong interest in education. As early as 1930, a Nez Perce, Archie Phinney, earned a doctoral degree from Columbia University. The tribal budget offers scholarship money for students, many of whom graduate from college with basic or advanced degrees. Nez Perces have become teachers, journalists, engineers, and doctors, nurses, and health care workers. Some work in the timber industry, in construction, or the military; others are truckers, farmers, or ranchers.

A young woman waves as she enters an arena to participate in one of the many events held each year to celebrate Nez Perce traditions.

Skilled Nez Perce artisans use modern art forms or traditional native designs, and continue to produce beautiful beaded jewelry and carrying bags.

The Nez Perce population has grown from about 1,400 in the 1950s to about 3,000. Nearly two thirds of these people live on or near the reservations.

Since the 1960s, there has been a renewed interest in Native American history. A sense of tribal identity among the Nez Perces and other Indian tribes has increased, along with a feeling of pride in their unique cultures.

Chief Joseph once said, "I know that my race must change. We cannot hold our own with the white men as we are." Today's leaders see the need for change, but they also respect Nez Perce traditions and values. Recently, Nez Perce leader Cliff Smith said, "For years we have been taught that the only way to succeed is to be white. We must reverse that kind of education and teach Indians to be Indians. Along with skills we must teach customs, traditions, languages, and treaties."

■ ■ ■

The Nez Perces made history in 1805 when they fed white explorers instead of harming them or turning them away. But these whites whom they treated as friends only led the way for others who took over their beloved lands. The Nez Perces survived war, disease, and the loss of their homelands as they moved into a new century and blended old ways with new. Their courage and the moving words of their great leaders stirred Americans in the 1800s and continue to inspire us today.

A NEZ PERCE CREATION STORY: THE HEART OF THE MONSTER

At the dawn of creation, there were no people on the earth, only animals. Elk, Grizzly Bear, Cottontail Rabbit, Rattlesnake, Eagle, and many others lived in the Kamiah Valley of present-day Idaho. But a fierce monster began to terrify the smaller animals in the valley. This beast, known as Ilt-swi-tsichs, was always hungry. To fill its huge stomach, it ate one animal after another.

The monster had gotten so large that it covered most of the valley. Old One sent his helper, Coyote, called *Iceye'eye*, to help the animals. When the monster saw Coyote, it wanted to eat him, too. Smacking its lips, it swallowed Coyote with a loud gulp. Down he went into the monster's stomach.

But clever Coyote was prepared. He had put five knives in his pocket. When he got near the monster's chest, he cut the heart away from its body, and the monster died. Quickly, Coyote climbed out of its mouth. He wanted to make sure the monster would never rise again, so he cut up its body. As he threw these pieces around, they became different groups of Indian peoples.

When he was done, Coyote realized he had not made any people to live in the Kamiah Valley. He squeezed blood from the monster's heart and mixed it with some water, then sprinkled it over the land. From that came the Nimipu (the people)—the Nez Perces. Nez Perce legend says that the place of creation, called the Heart of the Monster, is located on a slope in East Kamiah in Idaho.

IMPORTANT DATES

More than 10,000 years ago	The first settlers come to the Americas from Asia. The Nez Perces gradually settle in present-day Idaho, Oregon, and Washington and develop their traditional lifestyle.
1805	Lewis and Clark lead a group of explorers from St. Louis to the Pacific Coast and meet the Nez Perces in present-day Idaho.
1836	Henry and Eliza Spalding set up a mission at Lapwai on Nez Perce land.
1840	Young Joseph (later Chief Joseph) is born.
1855	The Walla Walla Treaty is signed opening much Indian land for white settlement.
1860	Miners rush to Nez Perce land after gold is found there.
1863	The so-called Thief Treaty is signed by about one-third of the Nez Perce chiefs; Old Joseph's Wallowa band is among those who refuse to sign.

1871	Old Joseph dies and his son, Young Joseph, becomes chief.
1874	The Nez Perces are told to move to the Lapwai Reservation in Idaho; they refuse.
1877	U.S. agents insist that the Wallowas and other Nez Perces move to the Lapwai Reservation. On the way, the Nez Perce War begins. Joseph surrenders on October 5 at the Bear Paws in Montana. His group is sent to North Dakota, then moved to Kansas, and later to Oklahoma.
1879	Joseph, now a famous Indian spokesman, visits Washington, D.C., to ask government leaders to let his group return to Idaho. His story about the Nez Perces' struggle is published in a magazine.
1885	Joseph and his band are sent to the Colville Reservation in Washington.
1904	Chief Joseph dies at the Colville Reservation; a monument is erected for him there the following year.
1924	The Snyder Act gives Native Americans full U.S. citizenship.
1934	The Indian Reorganization Act recognizes the rights of various tribes to form their own governments and religions.
1946	The Indian Claims Commission is set up.
1948	The Nez Perce tribe of Idaho becomes a self-governing body with its own constitution and bylaws.
1952	The Nez Perces file a claim to recover money for lands taken in violation of treaties and for gold that was removed from their land.
1959	The Indian Claims Commission rules in favor of the tribe, saying the government owes them nearly $20 million.
1965	Nez Perce National Historical Park in Idaho is founded.

GLOSSARY

Appaloosa. A spotted horse often bred and used by the Nez Perces.
Bitterroot. A pink-flowered plant gathered for food.
Camas. A blue-flowered member of the lily family; their starchy bulbs were a food staple for the Nez Perces.
Coyote (or Iceye'eye). A creature found in many Nez Perce legends; a helper to the Creator and sometimes a mischievous trickster.
Cradleboards. Padded wooden boards on which infants were strapped so that they could be carried from place to place.
Dreamer faith. A native religion that spread to the Nez Perces from the Columbia River tribes during the mid-1800s.
Hanyawat. The Creator, or Old One, in Nez Perce religious beliefs.
Ilt-swi-tsichs. The name of a monster in Nez Perce legend that once inhabited the ancestral land of the Kamiah Valley in Idaho.
Nimipu. The Nez Perce name for themselves; it means "the people" or "the real people."
Pithouse. A circular winter home built over a pit.
Sahaptin. The language group of the Nez Perces.
Sweathouse. A small building made of mud and grasses used for steam baths.
Ti-watitmas. A spirit helper.

BIBLIOGRAPHY

Books for children

Allard, William Albert. "Chief Joseph." *National Geographic*, March 1977.

Armstrong, Virginia I. *I Have Spoken: A Documentary History of Chief Joseph*. Athens, Ohio: Sage Books, 1971.

Beal, Merrill D. *I Will Fight No More Forever: Chief Joseph and the Nez Perce War*. Seattle: University of Washington Press, 1963.

*Britt, Albert. *Great Indian Chiefs*. New York: Dodd Mead, 1938.

*Brown, Mark H. *The Flight of the Nez Perce*. New York: G.P. Putnam's Sons, 1967.

*Davis, Russell. *Chief Joseph of the Nez Percé*. New York: McGraw-Hill, 1962.

Drury, Clifford M. *Henry Harmon Spalding*. Caldwell, Idaho: Caxton Printers, 1936.

Ellis, William S. "High Stepping Idaho." *National Geographic*, March 1973.

Gidley, M (Mick). *Kopet: A Documentary History of Chief Joseph's Last Years*. Seattle: University of Washington Press, 1981.

*Haines, Francis. *Indians of the Great Basin and Plateau*. New York: G.P. Putnam's Sons, 1970.

Haines, Francis. *The Nez Perces: Tribesmen of the Columbia Plateau.* Norman: University of Oklahoma Press, 1955.

*Heyman, William. *Famous American Indians.* New York: Dodd, Mead, 1972.

Hirsch, S. Carl. *Famous American Indians of the Plains.* New York: Rand McNally, 1973.

*Hofsinde, Robert. *The Indian and His Horse.* New York: Morrow, 1960.

Jackson, Donald, ed. *Letters of the Lewis and Clark Expedition With Related Documents 1783–1854.* Chicago: University of Chicago Press, 1962.

Josephy, Alvin M., Jr. *The Nez Perce Indians and the Opening of the Northwest.* New Haven, Conn.: Yale University Press, 1979.

Josephy, Alvin M., Jr., et al. *The Patriot Chiefs.* New York: Viking, 1961.

McDermott, John D. *Forlorn Hope: The Battle of White Bird Canyon and the Beginning of the Nez Perce War.* Boise: Idaho Historical Society, 1978.

McWhorter, Lucullus V. *Yellow Wolf: His Own Story.* Caldwell, Idaho: Caxton Printers, 1948.

*Nash, Gary B. *Red, White, and Black: The People of Early America.* Englewood Cliffs, N.J.: Prentice Hall, 1974.

*Osinksi, Alice. *The Nez Perce.* Chicago: Childrens Press, 1988.

*Place, Marian T. *Retreat to the Bear Paw: The Story of the Nez Perce.* New York: Four Winds, 1969.

Slickpoo, Allen P. *Noon Nee-Me-Poo (We, the Nez Perces).* Lapwai, Idaho: Nez Perce Tribe of Idaho, 1973.

Snyder, Gerald. *In the Footsteps of Lewis and Clark.* Washington, D.C.: National Geographic Society, 1970.

Spinden, Herbert Joseph. *The Nez Perce Indians.* New York: The American Anthropological Association, 1964.

Stevens, Hazard. *Life of Isaac Ingalls Stevens.* Boston: Houghton Miflin, 1904.

*Stirling, Matthew W. et al. *Indians of the Americas.* Washington, D.C.: National Geographic Society, 1959.

Vogel, Virgil J. *This Country Was Ours: A Documentary History of the American Indian.* New York: Harper & Row, 1972.

Walker, Deward E., Jr. *Indians of Idaho.* Moscow, Idaho: University Press of Idaho, 1978.

INDEX

Page numbers in *italics* refer to illustrations.

Appaloosa horse, 34

Bear Paws, Battle of, 10–11, 48
Blackfeet Indians, 37–38
Buffalo, 33, 34

Cayuse Indians, 12, 31
Children, 21–23, *22*, 25
Clark, William, 36–37
Clearwater River, 12, 16
Clothing, *27*
Columbia Plateau, 11, 15
Columbia River, 12, *16*, 31
Cradleboards, 21, *22*
Crafts, *33*

Diseases, 38
Dreamer faith, 44

Family life, 20–21
Fishing, 12, 23, 52, 53
Flathead Indians, 12, 31
Food, 12, 15, 16, 23–24, 26
Fur trade, 35, 38

Games, 24, 25
Gold, 43, 52
Guns, 37–38

Homes, 19
Horses, 31, 33–35
Household goods, 26, 28
Hunting, 26

Jefferson, Thomas, 36

Joseph, Chief, 9–11, 40, 43, 44, 45, 46–48, *49*, 50, 51, 55

Language, 12
Lewis, Meriwether, 36–37
Longhouses, 19
Louisiana Purchase, 35–36

Mandan Indians, 38
Manifest Destiny, 41
Missionaries, 39–40

Nez Perce Indians
   children, 21–23, *22*, 25
   clothing, *27*
   creation story, 56–57
   explorers and settlers and, 30, 35–44, *37*, 46, 55
   family life, 20–21
   food, 12, 15, 16, 23–24, 26
   games, 24, 25
   homes and property, 19–20
   horses, 31, 33–35
   household goods and tools, 26, 28
   language, 12
   modern, 51–55
   origin of name, 12
   reservations, 9, 11, 42, 43, 46, 47, 50, 52–53
   spiritual beliefs, 28–30, 44
   trade, 32–33, 35, 38
   tribal organization, 14, 17, *18*
   villages, 15–17
   women, 20–21
Nose ornament, 12, *14*

Ollokot, 11, 43

Palouse Indians, 12, 31
Pinecone games, 25
Pithouses, 19
Plains Indians, 12, 33
Plants, 24
Property, 19–20

Reservations, 9, 11, 42, 43, 46, 47, 50, 52–53

Sahaptin language, 12
Salmon River, 12, 16, 47
Shamans, 29
Shoshoni Indians, 12, 31
Sioux Indians, 33
Smith, Cliff, 55
Snake River, 12, *13*, 46
Spalding, Eliza, 40
Spalding, Henry, 40, *41*
Spiritual beliefs, 28–30, 44
Sweathouses, 19, *20*

Tipis, 34
Tools, 28
Trade, 32–33, 35, 38
Tribal organization, 14, 17, *18*
Tu-eka-kas, 40, 42, 43

Umatilla Indians, 12

Villages, 15–17
Vision quest, 29

Walla Walla Indians, 12, 31
Women, 20–21

Yakima Indians, 12, 31
Yellow Wolf, 10–11, 50